The Book of Medicines

T0165876

POEMS BY LINDA HOGAN

The Book of Medicines

COFFEE HOUSE PRESS :: MINNEAPOLIS :: 1993

Acknowledgments

Copyright © 1993 by Linda Hogan.

Cover art by Nora Koch.

Back cover photograph by Douglas Kent Hall.

Some of the poems in *The Book of Medicines* have appeared in: *Kenyon Review, Manoa, Ms. Magazine, Parabola, Plum Review, Red Dirt, American Voice, Mid-American Review, American Poetry Review.*

The author greatly acknowledges the following: Judy Grahn's "A Woman is Talking to Death," for line used in "History of Red"; Martha Graham's words— "house of pelvic truth"— used in "The Ritual Life of Animals"; Barbara Echols for inspiration for poem, "Two"; Eric Thomas for the rabbits huddled together in "Tear"; and to my friends, students, and relatives for growing ideas with me.

The publishers would like to thank the following funders for assistance which helped make this book possible: the Bush Foundation; the Dayton Hudson Foundation on behalf of Dayton's and Target Stores; The General Mills Foundation; The Lannan Foundation; The McKnight Foundation; The Andrew W. Mellon Foundation; The National Endowment for the Arts, a federal agency; The Beverly J. and John A. Rollwagen Fund of the Minneapolis Foundation; and Star and Tribune/Cowles Media Company. Major new marketing initiatives have been made possible by the Lila Wallace-Reader's Digest Literary Publisher's Marketing Development Prrogram, funded through a grant to the Council of Literary Magazine and Presses.

This activity is made possible in part by a grant provided by the Minnesota State Arts Board, through an appropriation by the Minnesota State Legislature.

Coffee House Press books are available to the trade through our primary distributor, Consortium Book Sales & Distribution, 1045 Westgate Drive, Saint Paul, MN 55114. Our books are also available through all major library distributors and jobbers, and through most small press distributors, including Bookpeople, Bookslinger, Inland, and Small Press Distribution. For personal orders, catalogs or other information, write to:

Coffee House Press
27 North Fourth Street, Suite 400 Minneapolis, MN 55401

LIBRARY OF CONGRESS CATALOGING IN PUBLICATION DATA

Hogan, Linda
    The Book of Medicines: poems/by Linda Hogan
    p. cm.
    ISBN-13: 978-1-56689-010-6
    ISBN-10: 1-56689-010-1
    1. Indians of North America—Poetry. 1. Title.
    PS3558.034726B66 1993
    811'.54—dc20   93-7677, CIP
    10 9 8 7 6 5 4

Contents

THE HISTORY OF RED

The History of Red

First
there was some other order of things
never spoken
but in dreams of darkest creation.

Then there was black earth,
lake, the face of light on water.
Then the thick forest all around
that light,
and then the human clay
whose blood we still carry
rose up in us
who remember caves with red bison
painted in their own blood,
after their kind.

A wildness
swam inside our mothers,
desire through closed eyes,
a new child
wearing the red, wet mask of birth,
delivered into this land
already wounded,
stolen and burned
beyond reckoning.

Red is this yielding land
turned inside out
by a country of hunters
with iron, flint and fire.
Red is the fear
that turns a knife back
against men, holds it at their throats,
and they cannot see the claw on the handle,
the animal hand

that haunts them
from some place inside their blood.

So that is hunting, birth,
and one kind of death.
Then there was medicine, the healing of wounds.
Red was the infinite fruit
of stolen bodies.
The doctors wanted to know
what invented disease
how wounds healed
from inside themselves
how life stands up in skin,
if not by magic.

They divined the red shadows of leeches
that swam in white bowls of water;
they believed stars
in the cup of sky,
They cut the wall of skin
to let
what was bad escape
but they were reading the story of fire
gone out
and that was a science.

As for the animal hand on death's knife,
knives have as many sides
as the red father of war
who signs his name
in the blood of other men.

And red was the soldier
who crawled
through a ditch
of human blood in order to live.
It was the canal of his deliverance.

It is his son who lives near me.
Red is the thunder in our ears
when we meet.
Love, like creation,
is some other order of things.

Red is the share of fire
I have stolen
from root, hoof, fallen fruit.
And this was hunger.

Red is the human house
I come back to at night
swimming inside the cave of skin
that remembers bison.
In that round nation
of blood
we are all burning,
red, inseparable fires
the living have crawled
and climbed through
in order to live
so nothing will be left
for death at the end.

This life in the fire, I love it,
I want it,
this life.

HUNGER

Fat

This is the land
where whales were mountains
pulled in by small boats,
where fat was rendered
out of darkness
by the light of itself,

where what fell through
the slaughtering decks
was taken in by land

until it became a hill made of fat
and blood, a town built on it.

The whale is the thick house of yesterday
in red waters.
It is the curve of another fortune,
a greasy smell and cloud
of dark smoke
that hides our faces.

At night
in this town
where hungers
are asleep,
we sleep
on a bed of secret fat.

A whale passes.
From dark strands of water,
it calls
its children by name,
Light, Smoke, Water, Land.

I hear it singing,
I sit up, awake.
It is a mountain rising,
lovely and immense.
I see myself
in the shine of it
and I want light.
I am full
with greed.
Give to me
light.

Hunger

Hunger crosses oceans.
It loses its milk teeth.
It sits on the ship and cries.

Thin, afraid,
it fashioned hooks to catch
the passing songs of whales so large
the men grew small
as distant, shrinking lands.
They sat on the ship and cried.

Hunger was the fisherman
who said dolphins are like women,
we took them from the sea
and had our way
with them.

Hunger knows we have not yet reached
the black and raging depths of anything.

It is the old man
who comes in the night
to cast a line
and wait at the luminous shore.
He knows the sea is pregnant
with clear fish
and their shallow pools of eggs
and that the ocean has hidden
signs of its own hunger,
lost men and boats
and squid that flew
toward churning light.

Hunger lives in the town
whose walls are made of shells

white and shining in the moon,
where people live surrounded
by what they've eaten
to forget that hunger
sits on a ship and cries.

And it is a kind of hunger
that brings us to love,
to rocking currents of a secret wave
and the body that wants to live beyond itself
like the destitute men
who took the shining dolphins from the sea.
They were like women,
they said,
and had their way
with them,
wanting to be inside,
to drink
and be held in
the thin, clear milk of the gods.

Bear Fat

When the old man rubbed my back
with bear fat
I dreamed the winter horses
had eaten the bark off trees
and the tails of one another.

I slept a hole into my own hunger
that once ate lard and bread
from a skillet seasoned with salt.

Fat was the light
I saw through
the eyes of the bear
three bony dogs leading men
into the grass-lined cave of sleep
to kill hunger
as it slept itself thin.

They grew fat
with the swallowed grease.
They ate even the wood-ashes
after the fire died
and when they slept,
did they remember back
to when they were wolves?

I am afraid of the future
as if I am the bear
turned in the stomach
of needy men
or the wolf become a dog
that will turn against itself
remembering what wildness was
before the crack of a gun,
before the men tried to kill it
or tame it
or tried to make it love them.

Return: Buffalo

One man made a ladder
of stacked-up yellow bones
to climb the dead
toward his own salvation.
He wanted
light and fire, wanted
to reach and be close to his god.

But his god was the one
who opened his shirt
and revealed the scar of mortal climbing.

It is the scar
that lives in the house with me.
It goes to work with me.
It is the people I have loved
who fell
into the straight, unhealed
line of history.
It is a brother
who heard the bellowing cry of sacred hills
when nothing was there
but stories and rocks.

It was what ghost dancers heard
in their dream
of bringing buffalo down from the sky
as if song and prayer
were paths life would follow back
to land.

And the old women, they say,
would walk that land,
pick through bones for hide, marrow,
anything that could be used

or eaten.
Once they heard a terrible moan
and stood back,
and one was not dead
or it had come back from there,
walked out of the dark mountains
of rotted flesh and bony fur,
like a prophet
coming out from the hills
with a vision
too unholy to tell.

It must have traveled the endless journey
of fear,
returned from the far reaches
where men believed the world was flat
and they would fall over
its sharp edge
into pitiless fire,

and they must have thought
how life came together
was a casual matter,
war a righteous sin,
and betrayal
wasn't a round, naked thing
that would come back to them
one day.

Harvesters of Night and Water

In night's broken waters
here is the boat,
white and small
with tiny men,
with impotent nets
limp as poverty
that when it ends
takes more than it needs.

In midnight
the circle of light in the boat
is filled with men and white arms,
with ropes moving like promise,
and nets pulling up the black and icy waters
a blue crab, tender inside its shell,
a star from another night of darkness than ours,
a glass-eyed halibut
so much larger than death
that the boatman must shoot it
and shoot again and in night,
fire flashes from the gun
like a flower that blooms
madness
and is gone.

Every yield is shining and alive,
and then at daybreak
the octopus,
the men pulling at it, but its many arms
fight hard, hold fast and tight
against the held boat,
in struggle with air and men,
holding as they scream. They want it.
They need it.
They are fighting.

It is a valuable thing.
It will be used as bait.
It will sell for two hundred dollars.
It will be cut into pieces,
will be taken
from the cut insides of halibut
and used again.
The men are still screaming,
fighting, but it cleaves to the white boat,
wearing the shine of water.

Its eyes do not look at the men
as they hook it with grappling hooks.
It faces the black, cold waters
it has been pulled from.
The tentacles fold over themselves
and inch down,
with the men screaming,
jabbing at it. I want to stop them.
I want to tell them what I know,
that this life collects coins
like they do
and builds walls on the floor of the sea.

It does not look at the men.
It does not see their need
rolling back above water,
the boat so white, so empty
even full.

And while water breathes up and back
it finds its way
into the ink black skin of water,
crossing other currents, floating
like a man's dream of falling
into worlds he will never know,
into the bending dark weeds
where rain lives

where crying lives,
where broken waters heal themselves.

I look inside the dark cold ocean.
Inside is the octopus that shone like sun
in a changing skin of water.
It turned red with fear, then paled before
climbing down the boat.
It was naked,
it was beautiful
like an angel
with other wings,
its arms were those of four mothers
desperate for life.

My child saw a tentacle come
over the boat.
She is the girl who loves fish;
she kissed one once.
She doesn't understand death.
She has not knocked on its door the way I have.
She does not know the world is made of arms.
She keeps the lens of the halibut eye,
looks through the perfect glass sphere
and sees the wide curving world
all at once.

Hungry, we are hungry for the whole world.
We are like the small fish in the sea,
the ones who swim into the mouths of larger ones
to take what's there.

I want the world to be kinder.
I am a woman.
I am afraid.
I saw a star once, falling toward me.
It was red
with brilliant arms
and then it was gone.

Bear

For Smoke
For Hawk

The bear is a dark continent
that walks upright
like a man.

It lives across the thawing river.
I have seen it
beyond the water,
beyond comfort. Last night
it left a mark at my door
that said winter
was a long and hungry night of sleep.
But I am not afraid; I have collected
other nights of fear,
knowing what things walked
the edges of my sleep,

and I remember
the man who shot
a bear,
how it cried like he did
and in his own voice,
how he tracked that red song
into the forest's lean arms
to where the bear lay weeping
on fired earth,
its black hands
covering its face from sky
where humans believe god lives
larger than death.

That man,
a madness remembers him.
It is a song in starved shadows
in nights of sleep.
It follows him.
Even the old rocks sing it.
It makes him want
to get down on his knees
and lay his own hands
across his face and turn away
from sky where god lives
larger than life.

Madness is its own country,
desperate and ruined.
It is a collector of lives.
It's a man
afraid of what he's done
and what he lives by. Safe,
we are safe
from the bear
and we have each other,
we have each other
to fear.

Mountain Lion

She lives on the dangerous side
of the clearing
in the yellow-eyed shadow of a darker fear.
We have seen each other
inside mortal dusk,
and what passed between us
was the road
ghosts travel
when they cannot rest
in the land of the terrible other.
Red spirits of hunters
walked between us
from the place where blood
goes back to its wound
before fire
before weapons.
Nothing was hidden
in our eyes.
I was the wild thing
she had learned to fear.
Her power lived
in a dream of my leaving.
It was the same way
I have looked so many times at others
in clear light
before lowering my eyes
and turning away
from what lives inside those
who have found
two worlds cannot live
inside a single vision.

Crossings

There is a place at the center of earth
where one ocean dissolves inside the other
in a black and holy love;
It's why the whales of one sea
know songs of the other,
why one thing becomes something else
and sand falls down the hourglass
into another time.

Once I saw a fetal whale
on a block of shining ice.
Not yet whale, it still wore the shadow
of a human face, and fingers
that had grown before the taking
back and turning into fin.
It was a child from the curving world
of water turned square,
cold, small.

Sometimes the longing in me
comes from when I remember
the terrain of crossed beginnings
when whales lived on land
and we stepped out of water
to enter our lives in air.

Sometimes it's from the spilled cup of a child
who passed through all the elements
into the human fold,
but when I turned him over
I saw that he did not want to live
in air. He'd barely lost
the trace of gill slits
and already he was a member of the clan of crossings.
Like tides of water,
he wanted to turn back.

I spoke across elements
as he was leaving
and told him, Go.
It was like the wild horses
that night when fog lifted.
They were swimming across the river.
Dark was that water,
darker still the horses,
and then they were gone.

Breaking

Water grew between two lands
that once were one.
That was the first breaking,
and the stories in each grain of sand,
older than we are,
come apart,
not even a trace of the first ones,
no jawbone turning over
in the great salt of blood and brine,
no finger, mountain
or splinter of leg.
How does water do it,
strip a world to its bones,
how does it dance that way
without feet,
sing without a voice,
caress with no hands
and follow the moon
without a single eye?

Crow Law

The temple where crow worships
walks forward in tall, black grass.
Betrayal is crow's way of saying grace
to the wolf
so it can eat
what is left
when blood is on the ground,
until what remains of moose
is crow
walking out
the sacred temple of ribs
in a dance of leaving
the red tracks of scarce and private gods.
It is the oldest war
where moose becomes wolf and crow,
where the road ceases
to become the old forest
where crow is calling,
where we are still afraid.

Skin

The men wore human skins
but removed them at night
and fell to the bottom of darkness
like crows without wings.

War was the perfect disguise.
Their mothers would not have known them,
and the swarming flies could not find them.
When they met a spirit in the forest
it thought they were bags of misfortune
and walked away
without taking their lives.

In this way,
they tricked the deer
that wandered into the forest at night,
thinking branches of trees
were other deer.

If I told you the deer was a hide
of light, you wouldn't believe it,
or that it was a hunting song
that walked out of a diviner's bag
sewn from human skin.
It knew it could pass
through the bodies of men and return.
It knew the arrow belonged to the bow,
and that men only think they are following
the deaths of animals
or other men
when they are walking
into the fire.

That's why fire is restless
and smoke has become
the escaped wings of crows,
why war is only another skin,
and why men are just the pulled back curve of the bow.

Salt

Salt is the rich world
that skirts all bodies
of land and skin.
It lives in the swaying ghost of ocean
that flew to the sky.
Under rain's soft hands it gave way
like love
between a woman and a man.
It was the taste of skin,
it was life gathered into semen, egg,
the seed of a child,
the first sweat of labor.
It was the child's black hair,
wet and crowning.
It was the mother's weeping.
It was the beautiful child grown to full life,
the child fed on deer meat.
It was what the mother became, looking back
at what she'd left behind,
the pale blue houses
on an empty street.
She was turned into tears.
She was the woman who was dying of thirst,
held afloat in the salt sea.
The surgeon poured it on her wound.
It seared the poor flesh.
The chemist tried to burn it.
It became a white dry edge of sadness.
It drew the living deer to danger.
Salt, I hate you,
how you sting.
You don't cry,
you are cried,
the way I don't live
but am lived.

Shelter

Tonight the walls are only thin, dead trees
of a felled world that stands again
between this body and the stars.

Downstairs, my daughter sleeps.
There is only a thin, closed eyelid
between her and all the rest.
A dream
I am to her.
She doesn't know my sorrows or passion.
I am just large and dark,
the woman who feeds her,
but now, her body grows beyond her
and wants to make life of its own,
to let new worlds fall from her
like dark water through a tribal hand.

She believes she is safe
in the shadows of this house
and what's above us both.
Once I told her about my cousin.
On a rainy day
a man took him to a cave
in order to hurt him.
She did not believe me,
she is such a dreamer,
and she doesn't believe in god.

At the shore
there is a quiet bird.
It stands on one leg.
Blue fish hover in its shadow
believing they are safe
in dark shade
that will bend and swallow them.

Bamboo

First woman was made of slender bones
like these that stand upright together
in the rich, green world of daylight.

At night, they are a darkened forest
of sisters who grow quickly
in moving water
and talk in the clattering breeze
as if each is an open throat, rising
to speak.

I tell a man about this beautiful,
creaking world, how it flowers all
at once. He has been to war. He says
with bamboo they do terrible things
to men and women.

I look at this bamboo.
It did not give permission to soldiers.
It is imprisoned in its own skin.
The stalks are restless about this.
They have lived too long in the world of men.
They are hollow inside.

Lord, are you listening to this?
Plants are climbing to heaven
to talk to you.

Map

This is the world
so vast and lonely
without end, with mountains
named for men
who brought hunger
from other lands,
and fear
of the thick, dark forest of trees
that held each other up,
knowing fire dreamed of swallowing them
and spoke an older tongue,
and the tongue of the nation of wolves
was the wind around them.
Even ice was not silent.
It cried its broken self
back to warmth.
But they called it
ice, wolf, forest of sticks,
as if words would make it something
they could hold in gloved hands,
open, plot a way
and follow.

This is the map of the forsaken world.
This is the world without end
where forests have been cut away from their trees.
These are the lines wolf could not pass over.
This is what I know from science:
that a grain of dust dwells at the center
of every flake of snow,
that ice can have its way with land,
that wolves live inside a circle
of their own beginning.
This is what I know from blood:
the first language is not our own.

There are names each thing has for itself,
and beneath us the other order already moves.
It is burning.
It is dreaming.
It is waking up.

Drought

Once we said thunder
was the old man of sky snoring,
lightning was the old man
striking a match,
but now we only want him to weep
so we tell him our stories
in honest tongues.

Naming the Animals

After the words that called legs, hands,
the body
of man out of clay and sleep,
after the forgotten voyages of his own dreaming,
the forgotten clay of his beginnings,
after nakedness and fear of something larger,
these he named; wolf, bear, other
as if they had not been there
before his words, had not
had other tongues and powers
or sung themselves into life
before him.

These he sent crawling into wilderness
he could not enter,
swimming into untamed water.
He could hear their voices at night
and tracks and breathing
at the fierce edge of forest
where all things know the names for themselves
and no man speaks them
or takes away their tongue.

His children would call us pigs.
I am a pig,
the child of pigs,
wild in this land
of their leavings,
drinking from water that burns
at the edge of a savage country
of law and order.
I am naked, I am old
before the speaking,
before any Adam's forgotten dream,
and there are no edges to the names,

no beginning, no end.
From somewhere I can't speak or tell,
my stolen powers
hold out their hands
and sing me through.

The Fallen

It was the night
a comet with its silver tail
fell through darkness
to earth's eroded field,
the night I found
the wolf,
starved in metal trap,
teeth broken
from pain's hard bite,
its belly swollen with unborn young.

In our astronomy
the Great Wolf
lived in sky.
It was the mother of all women
and howled her daughter's names
into the winds of night.

But the new people,
whatever stepped inside their shadow,
they would kill,
whatever crossed their path,
they came to fear.

In their science,
Wolf was not the mother.
Wolf was not wind.
They did not learn healing
from her song.

In their stories
Wolf was the devil, falling
down an empty,
shrinking universe,
God's Lucifer

with yellow eyes
that had seen their failings
and knew that they could kill the earth,
that they would kill each other.

That night
I threw the fallen stone back to sky
and falling stars
and watched it all come down
to ruined earth again.

Sky would not take back
what it had done.

That night, sky was a wilderness so close
the eerie light of heaven
and storming hands of sun
reached down the swollen belly
and dried up nipples of a hungry world.

That night,
I saw the trapper's shadow
and it had four legs.

The Ritual Life of Animals

The animal walks beside me,
long-toothed partner
in a sacrificial dance.
It lies down on the land
as I walk upright.
It has come from the swampy beginnings
of blood, lung, hand.
Killing is the prayer
before its every meal.
And in the dark nocturnal waking,
there's the falling
to all fours, a wild seeing,
other ears hearing.

After breathing and clawing,
is the solemn rite of sleep
that crosses
into dream,
that holds
council with foreign tongues
and common hungers.
In the sleeping bird,
the dream is flying south.
The male
is the dance before the female,
and there is fear; I am the enemy
dreamed in the restless sleep of whale,
bird, those who possess
the desperate gifts
of feigning death, running,
turning the color of snow.

In the silence
of night,
in the warmth of human bodies,

are the nocturnal wakings.
Something inside gets down on its haunches.
At the borders of our beds
are the strange ways, voices,
the slow shifting of eyes, turning of ears.
They hear us, smell us, dream us.
We lie down
in the long nights of their waking,
the world of animal law,
the house of pelvic truth.

Travelers

The terrible cold
is a closing hand.
It takes back the edges of land and water
it once offered.

It is alive,
you mustn't doubt this,
and it holds danger in its fist.
It says a mirage
is a city of warmth,
but when you go there
it is always beyond
the next white horizon
that can never be possessed.

I was looking at that far city
the night snow lied
about the darker world beneath it,
that brittle night
it grew cold so fast
the geese froze into water
and couldn't fly.
Their fear cried out
across the helpless land,
and when I heard them
I was the hand of death gone soft
enough to hit the solid skin of water
with stick, with rock,
with fear that what held them
held me.

South was their way that night.
They wanted to follow it.
Even my human ears heard its blue voice
in the stretched and beating wings,

as I cut one leg loose, then another,
until breaking gave way
to currents above and below
that drew them. They pushed
against the broken edges of water,
long-necked angels that rose,
escaping me and ice
and sky took them in
beyond the curved edge of horizon
where one beautiful world
moved above another
skimming the flat white lake,
the wounded ice
left behind to heal itself.

Tracking

After a long season of rains
we followed the wild pig,
its hoofprints like small arrows
through dark moss and ferns,
to borrow its sharp-backed life
for a while
inside our own.

It pawed the wet ground
for milk-white potatoes
that filled themselves
beneath the ground.

In the dark forest it went,
where growing sticks
were sharp as the black,
wounded heart of brush,
where roads ended in fog,
where the first race of men
built walls of small, white stones
that have not fallen,
then vanished
into the dark center of things
that beats like a heart
unable to cry
back the old lives,
the uncertain lands and tongues.

We followed the tracks like arrows
into a cave
where the walls were wet and shining
but they did not come out
and no pig was there,
only cool emptiness.

We hoped it was not an angry ghost
or hungry
or lonely
but the damp black stones were shining
in there
and on the ceiling
were painted the green birds
that once lived
in the rain and the trees.

It was like the night
I woke beneath the river
and there was no way back to the forest
except to become a spring of clear water,
to fill myself
and make a new way
through the world.

Milk

At night
inside the steamed windows
of the milk barn,
the milking machines are at work,
steel amidst the animal warmth
of cattle, nipples just washed,
brought in from the field.

I remember the smell of my mother's milk,
the taste of beginnings
when she was food for another child.
I am a body
grown from nipple,
from when we were
sharers of the same body,
one lost
in the waters of the other.

Milk is the beginning of a journey
that opens into other journeys,
cattle brought in the dark
holds of ships
from other bodies of land,
across waters.
They were hungry,
with angled bones
poking through the darkness
where they stood,
ate, weakened,
coupled and gave birth afraid
their kind would not go on,
and the milk sellers
hoisting up the dying
thirsty cow
too weak to stand

in leather straps and milking death,
drinking its watery milk,
eating land,
they were hungry.

At the river one day
the women were washing cloth
blue as the flowing light of milk.
It could have been stolen by water,
carried away, except for the hands that held it.
Something must hold me this way,
and you,
and the thin blue tail of the galaxy,
to keep us from leaving
as life unfolds behind us
over long roads and intricate, human waters.

THE BOOK OF MEDICINES

The Alchemists

By day
they bent over lead's
heavy spirit of illness,
asking it to be gold,
the lord from humble beginnings.

And the mad soul of mercury
fell through their hands
through settled floors
and came to rest
silver and deadly
in a hidden corner
where it would grow.

Gold was the property
that could take sickness out
from lead.
It was fire
held still.
At night
they lifted the glass
of black grapes
and sugar to their lips
and drank the flaked gold
suspended in wine
like sparks of fire,
then watched it fall
like fool's gold
to the bottom of a pond.

Yesterday, my father behind a curtain
in the sick ward
heard a doctor
tell a man where the knife
would cut flesh.

Listen, my father said,
that man is saying a poem.
No, he's telling a story.
No, I believe
he is reading from a magical book.

But he was only a man
talking to iron,
willing it to be gold.

If it had worked
we would kneel down before it
and live forever,
all base metals
in ceremonial fire.

The Grandmother Songs

The grandmothers were my tribal gods.
They were there
when I was born. Their songs
rose out of wet labor
and the woman smell of birth.

From a floating sleep
they made a shape around me,
a grandmother's embrace,
the shawl of family blood
that was their song for kinship.

There was a divining song
for finding the lost,
and a raining song
for the furrow and its seed,
one for the hoe
and the house it leaned against.

In those days, through song,
a woman could fly
to the mother of water
and fill her ladle
with cool springs of earth.

She could fly to the deer
and sing him down to the ground.

Song was the pathway where people met
and animals crossed.

Once, flying out of the false death of surgery,
I heard a grandmother singing for help.
She came close
as if down a road of screaming.

It was a song I never knew
lived inside the muscle
of this common life.

It was the terror grandmother.
I'd heard of her.
And when our fingers and voices met,
the song
of an older history came through
my mouth.

At death, they say
everything inside us opens,
mouth, heart, even the ear opens
and breath passes
through the memories
of loves and faces.
The embrace opens
and grandmothers pass,
wearing sunlight
and thin rain,
walking out of fire
as flame
and smoke
leaving the ashes.

That's when rain begins,
and when the mouth of the river sings,
water flows from it
back to the cellular sea
and along the way
earth sprouts and blooms, the grandmothers
keep following the creation
that opens before them
as they sing.

Tear

It was the time before
I was born.
I was thin.
I was hungry. I was
only a restlessness inside a woman's body.

Above us, lightning split open the sky.
Below us, wagon wheels cut land in two.
Around us were the soldiers,
young and afraid,
who did not trust us
with scissors or knives
but with needles.

Tear dresses they were called
because settler cotton was torn
in straight lines
like the roads we had to follow
to Oklahoma.

But when the cloth was torn,
it was like tears,
impossible to hold back,
and so they were called
by this other name,
for our weeping.

I remember the women.
Tonight they walk
out from the shadows
with black dogs,
children, the dark heavy horses,
and worn-out men.

They walk inside me. This blood
is a map of the road between us.
I am why they survived.
The world behind them did not close.
The world before them is still open.
All around me are my ancestors,
my unborn children.
I am the tear between them
and both sides live.

Tear dresses are traditional Chickasaw women's clothing.

Chambered Nautilus

It's from before the spin of human fire,
before the dreaming that grew out of itself,
before there were people who ate the brains
of the dead,
before wind was leaving through a hole in the sky,
before zero and powers of ten,
before nets drifting the empty miles of water,
from when moon was the only tyrant that ruled the sea
and was the god shells rose to at night,
the builder of chambers,
the geometry of light, even infinity
is shaped this way
and the curve of sea lives in it,
the unwritten laws of water,
and it still rises
to the surface of darkness,
the country of drifting,
seeking a new kind of light to live inside,
from when we were less savage than now,
when shells were barter for corn
and cloth, and mirrors,
and we built dwellings of stone.
We were strong.
We were full.
Europeans did not powder our bones
and drink them, believing their powers
would grow
and there were no torturers leaving stone prisons
at night to buy bread and sugar
for their wives.
It was before there were bear-slayers
and slayers of women and land
and belief. We knew earth was a turtle
swimming between stars
and everything that was savage in us

fought to the quick
because everything that lived had radiance
like the curve of water and shell
of whatever animal
still inside
that has brought me here.

Sickness

If we are all one,
then in my hand
is the mortal enemy,
the one that felled the forest,
struck the fire,
the doctors of torture
living at the edge of sanity
that, like broken glass,
does not call itself sharp.

In sickness are the stories of a broken world.
It is the wedged cut in a tree,
the strike between match and wood.
It is the way children of burned deer
walk out of the fire.

I am the child of humans,
I have witnessed their destruction inside myself,
and crawled along the ground
among fallen trees
and long grasses. Down there,
I saw disease.
It closed doors, turned on light.
It owned water and land.
It believed in its country
and followed orders.
It went to work.
It tried to take my tongue.
But these words,
these words are proof
there is healing.

Carry

From water's broken mirror
we pulled it,
alive and shining,
gasping the painful other element of air.
It was not just fish.
There was more.
It was hawk, once wild with
hunger, sharp talons
locked into the dying twist
and scale of fish,
its long bones
trailing like a ghost
behind fins
through the dark, cold water.

It was beautiful, that water,
like a silver coin stretched thin
enough to feed us all,
smooth as skin before anyone knew
the undertow's rough hands
lived inside it, working everything down
to its absence,
and water is never lonely,
it holds so many.
It says, come close, you who want to swallow me;
already I am part of you.
Come near. I will shape myself around you
so soft, so calm
I will carry you
down to a world you never knew or dreamed,
I will gather you
into the hands of something stronger,
older, deeper.

Glass

When I was a child
I would stand between mirrors
and see myself grow small,
infinite
and far away.

I didn't know the ancestors'
lives had been traded
for the vision of our faces
inside our own hands.

I didn't know I would someday drink
the fermented
body of another god
and become the color of holes
in danger of breaking.

A mirror is such a circle
of revelations.

It is the place wind blows through
when winter enters the room,
the wounded place
Raven walked out from,
believing his feathers were white
until he saw himself
black and shining
above the gray water and wilderness
we lived inside and long for,
the way glass wants to go back
to being sand
and ice wants to return
to being water on earth
as it is in heaven.
This life,

it's like living in water,
in the cracks between thawing ice
that has begun to live again,
where seals come up for breath,
where sky sees
the skin of another self
all the infinite way down
to where breaking and darkness
are simple powers.

The Bricks

Their ancestors came from the muddy gulches
where wild gourds grew.
Salamanders lived there,
and snakes
in other skins,
and desperate seeds
afloat at the edge of forest
that settled in with clay,
slipping through
the architect's plans
the way life breaks through
the stonemason's love
and enters the world in a woman.

There is a secret longing
inside bricks that hold worlds
together, a forest dreaming
inside every wall,
wanting to send out
a passionate tendril of life,
as in Japan
when humans emptied other humans
of their lives.
Cities fell
and bricks flowered
with plants from distant mountains.

Old people used to say
some of us entered this world on a vine
like yellow gourds
and we will climb another
into the next.
In those days
we were marvelous children of clay
rocking in the mud mother's lap.

The fine-boned wind
breathed through us.
We did not yet
live inside walls of bricks,
we did not know destruction would bloom
or the world would live beyond us,
that clay would stand upright,
knowing a forest lived inside it,
and rain
and fire.

Drum

Inside the dark human waters
of our mothers,
inside the blue drum of skin
that beat the slow song of our tribes
we knew the drifts of continents
and moving tides.

We are the people who left water
to enter a dry world.
We have survived soldiers and drought,
survived hunger
and living
inside the unmapped terrain
of loneliness.
That is why we have thirst.
It is why
when we love
we remember our lives in water,
that other lives fall through us
like fish swimming in an endless sea,
that we are walking another way
than time,
to new life, backward
to deliver ourselves to rain and river,
this water
that will become other water
this blood that will become other blood
and is the oldest place
the deepest world
the skin of water
that knows the drum before a hand meets it.

Skin Dreaming

Skin is the closest thing to god,
touching oil, clay,
intimate with the foreign land of air
and other bodies,
places not in light,
lonely
for its own image.

It is awash in its own light.
It wants to swim and surface
from the red curve of sea,
open all its eyes.

Skin is the oldest thing.
It remembers when it was the cold
builder of fire,
when darkness was the circle around it,
when there were eyes shining in the night,
a breaking twig, and it rises
in fear, a primitive lord on new bones.

I tell you, it is old,
it heals and is sometimes merciful.
It is water.
It has fallen through ancestral hands.
It is the bearer of vanished forest
fallen through teeth and jaws
of earth
where we were once other
visions and creations.

Partings

Torn from her far beginnings,
the moon was once earth,
a daughter whose leaving broke land to pieces.
Here is the scar of rupture,
this ocean of ancient rain
that still rises
and falls with the moon's turning dance
around her mother.

This is what it means to be mother and child,
to wear the skin of ancestors,
the mother's stolen lands
carried on the face of the other.

Earth tells her,
return all lies to their broken source,
trust in the strange science of healing.
Believe the medicine of your own hand.
Believe that emptiness is the full
dance between us
and let it grow.

It is a road of deliverance
sure as the path Moses pulled
between the red, uncertain waters
and others followed.

Think of the place
where a continent divides
and water falls away from itself.

Think of the midwife
whose knife made two lives
where there was only one.
She had mastered the way
of beautiful partings.

It is true our lives
will betray us in the end
but life knows where it is going,
so does water,
so does blood,
and the full and endless dance of space.

Gather

We sat inside and sewed.
We gathered our skirts,
pulling cloth
along the thread.

It was raining.
The cotton plants were drowning.
We wanted the sky to close,
wanted a dry hot wind
to pull water back up the sky,
a wick to the hot light of sun,
to let the plants breathe, grow,
be picked.

It's in the stars, my mother said,
that bloom pale and soft
behind the rain,
even if cotton can't.

She was a faith healer, of sorts.
By that, I mean she always held a cure
for hopelessness, could lay a hand
on misery and make it smile,
like when the old German
came to collect the rent.
He was beneath a black umbrella
while she stood in the rain.
Through the fogged window
I watched her
give him one of the rabbits
that sat together in a warm huddle
and when he left, I couldn't tell
her tears from the rain,
but she raised her arms
and loved the rain and sky.

She didn't need a skirt, I thought,
she had her own skin.
And once she'd said, Remember
the gods wear seamless garments.

Two

The weight of a man on a woman
is like falling into the river without drowning.

Above, the world is burning and fighting.
Lost worlds flow through others.

But down here beneath water's skin,
river floor, sand, everything

is floating, rocking.
Water falls through our hands as we fall through it.

And when a woman and a man come up from water
they stand at the elemental edge of difference.

Mirrored on water's skin,
they are fired clay, water evaporating into air.

They are where water turns away from land
and goes back to enter a larger sea.

A man and a woman are like those rivers,
entering a larger sea

greater than the sum of all its parts.

Nothing

Nothing sings in our bodies
like breath in a flute.
It dwells in the drum.
I hear it now
that slow beat
like when a voice said to the dark,
let there be light,
let there be ocean
and blue fish
born of nothing
and they were there.
I turn back to bed.
The man there is breathing.
I touch him
with hands already owned by another world.
Look, they are desert,
they are rust. They have washed the dead.
They have washed the just born.
They are open.
They offer nothing.
Take it.
Take nothing from me.
There is still a little life
left inside this body,
a little wildness here
and mercy
and it is the emptiness
we love, touch, enter in one another
and try to fill.

Gate

A man thinks he is a window
standing clear and upright,
already one with sky
but he is only looking out
at what he wants,
sons in a world of plenty,
a body that will never break.

A woman believes she is a door,
wood from the ancient forest.
When it's safe she can open,
welcome the man
or go outside
and harvest the rich, dark plants.

A child dreams she is a wall
holding window and door together.
She will never go hungry
or sleep in sinful beds.

In town, nearby, the people stand
at a gate, closed inside
the unhinged emptiness
and look at endless dark,
at the ones who milk cows
with long fingers.
They believe the gods live far
beyond a latched gate of night,
among grapevines and silver wheat,
where the scale
never tips with the weight
of a butcher's hand.

They think heaven is so far away,
beyond the farthest towns,

not beneath the mortal sky,
not the radiant fields of potatoes
brown with dust,
not the gold-eyed eagle perched
in a tree,
with perfect feathers and bones of air,
and not where children are born,
through the body's gate of mystery,
red and crying.

And farther out,
there's a vast blue sea
with great, turning fish
and holy rains
dissolving, coming together
with land.

The Direction of Light

New stones have risen up earth's labor
toward air. Everything rises,
the ocean in a cloud,
the rain forest passing
above our heads.
Children grow inch by inch
like trees in a graveyard,
victors over the same gravity
that pulls us down.
Even our light continues
on through the universe, and do we stop to
wonder who will see it
and where,
when the light of this earth is gone?
May there long be our light.

And then it falls. Shades are pulled down
between two worlds, clouds fall
as rain, light returns
the way rain from Brazil falls
in New York and the green parrots
in their cages feel it, shake their
feathers, and remember home
and are alive
and should they be thankful
for that gift
or should they curse like sailors and grieve?

I tell the parrots,
I too have wanted to give up
on everything
when what was right turned wrong
and the revolutionaries
who rose up
like yeast in life's bread, turned
against those who now rise up.

That's why I take the side of light—
don't you?— with the weight of living
tugging us down and earth wanting us back
despite great thoughts and smiling faces
that are prisons in between
the worlds of buying
and selling even the parrots
we teach to say "Hello."

Hello. Did I call this poem
the direction of light?
I meant *life*
so let this word
overthrow the first
and rise up to the start.

Great Measures

The first time a lover held me
I was young
and gave myself
to creation.
I was hand, body, liquid
ruled by dark seas
that swallow the edges of land
and give them up to another place.

I am still this measure of brine,
ancient carbon, the pull of iron
across linked and desperate distances,
beginning and end together
the way sunlight on skin
is still connected
to the fiery storms of its origins.

I'm thinking this today,
candling eggs
to see inside the oval light
which yolks are quickened
with a spot of blood.
Once these were wilder birds
who would go to any lengths
to follow the magnetic longings
of stars.

Oh, makers of eggs,
this living is such a journey
inside a breaking open world,
the way a turtle free of its shell
believes in water,
getting its bearings
across the stretch of sand,
that distance to dark water,

breaking, gaining, running
for shelter,
but when it swims,
it remembers the sand
it is ruled by.

Other, Sister, Twin

She began with two lovers
on the swept floor of earth.

She was what passed between them.

She was a gourd too heavy for the vine
and full of her own wet seed.

Her grandmother kept the red bag
that held her stem
so she would not forget
the other women she lived inside
before this ruined time.

The beginning of hunger
was in that bag
with bones and the origins of betrayal,
but there was the forgiving thing,
the dry seeds of the rattle
that could shake healing to a start.

She stood naked
and painted herself
in the old way,
a red hand
across her face.
She danced in the ceremony
of fire
that rose to the stars.
She wrapped night's black skin
around her shoulders
and disappeared inside its dance.

She is the one that lives now
in the hand of the river

that wants to flow away from itself
but never does,
and at night she falls
beneath the water
where once I woke wearing her painted skin.
The red hand of it was on me.
I knew I was water
and heard her say,
Above is the betrayed world
where our children are the children of strangers
along the lost road
in the land where barns are red
because they are painted with the blood and milk
of mothers
of what they hold.

The closed bundles of healing
are beginning to open.

The first stem is growing like a vine.

It holds the cure
where you can reach through time
and find the bare earth
within your living hand.

I say her name.
It is earth calling land,
Mother.

It is glacier calling ice,
My daughter, my sister.

It is ocean
calling the river,
Water.

Flood: The Sheltering Tree

In rain's dark, unreal night
I stand on the mound
beneath the only tree.
Water rises.
The calves have no choice
but to join me,
though they know I am the shadow
of the knife
at their necks
and we stand in the bones
of their mothers.

Land takes back the forgotten name of rain
and speaks it
like a roar, dark and running
away from breaking sky.

Where will it take us, time, water,
the uneasy slope of this land
that runs from itself
and thins into other lands
crossing empty space we've cried in,
washed down to the wound,
when we were crowded too long,
and began to see again
the beautiful unwinding field
and remember our lives
from before the time of science,
before we fell from history,

and the rain is old men, bent and dancing.
I know their wet song. It is thunder.
It is sage, stripped down to the warm smell of healing.
It carries me down
to its yearning dream of tides

with red turtles swimming in it,
dark turtles, old and silent
with yellow, open eyes.

The Origins Of Corn

This is the female corn.
This is the male.
These are the wild skirts flying
and here is the sweet dark daughter
that passed between those
who were currents of each other's love.
She sleeps
in milky sweetness. She is the stranger
that comes from a remote land, another time
where sky and earth are lovers always
for the first time each day,
where crops begin to stand
amid brown dry husks, to rise straight
and certain as old people with yellowed hair
who carry medicines,
the corn song,
the hot barefoot dance
that burns your feet
but you can't stop
trading gifts
with the land,
putting your love in the ground
so that after the long sleep of seeds
all things will grow
and the plants who climb into this world
will find it green and alive.